Cascarones Are for Fun

by Sammie Witt
illustrated by Sue Frankenberry

PEARSON

Scott
Foresman

Editorial Offices: Glenview, Illinois • Parsippany, New Jersey • New York, New York
Sales Offices: Needham, Massachusetts • Duluth, Georgia • Glenview, Illinois
Coppell, Texas • Ontario, California • Mesa, Arizona

What Are Cascarones?

See the eggshells in the picture? These special eggshells are called *cascarones*. Cascarones is a Spanish word that means "shells." You say the word like this: kas-ka-ron-nez.

In this book you will find out about cascarones and why they are so much fun.

3

The cascarones look pretty, don't they? Would you be surprised to learn that people are supposed to break them? And they not only break them, but they break them over one another's heads!

But don't worry. No real egg will get on people's heads. Cascarones are made with just the eggshells.

4

In Mexico and parts of the United States, people use cascarones to **celebrate** special days.

On those days, children love to surprise friends and family by cracking the cascarones over their heads. No one gets mad when the eggs are broken over them. They are grateful because the eggshells and the stuff inside bring good luck.

5

How Are Cascarones Made?

Here is a family making cascarones. First, they make small holes in both ends of an egg. Then, they blow the raw egg from inside the shell out into a bowl.

Afterward, they clean the eggshells with water and let them safely dry.

When the empty eggshells are ready, people **decorate** the shells by painting them.

6

After the paint is dry, the cascarones are filled with **confetti** and small toys. Confetti is tiny pieces of colored paper. The confetti flies out when the eggshells are cracked open.

7

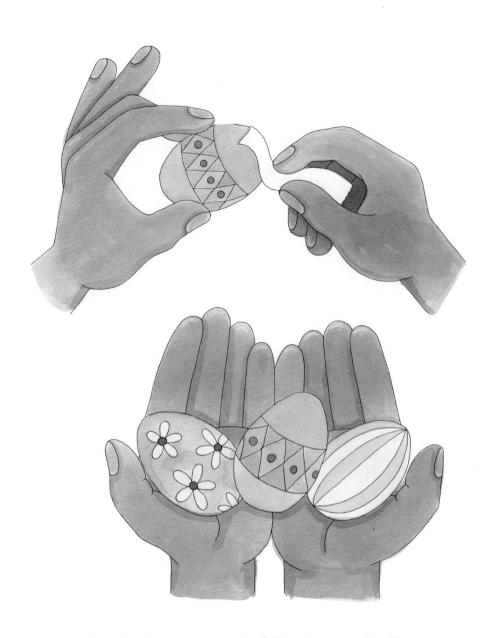

The holes in each filled eggshell are closed with a small piece of tape.

Now the cascarones are ready for the celebration—and so are the people who made them!

Who Brought the First Cascarones?

Long ago, there was a famous explorer named Marco Polo. He was from **Italy**.

Marco Polo went all over the world and brought many things back from his travels.

One of the things he brought back were special eggs from **China**. These eggs were like cascarones. But they were not filled with confetti. They were filled with **perfume** or powder.

9

These eggs became popular in Italy. Young men would toss the eggs to young women. Sometimes the eggs broke, and the woman would get covered in the perfume or powder.

Other countries soon came to **cherish** the filled eggs as well.

The idea of these special eggs was brought to **Mexico** by the **Empress** Carlotta. She and her husband ruled Mexico more than 150 years ago.

Some say that Empress Carlotta was the first person who had the eggshells filled with confetti instead of perfume and powder.

When Are Cascarones Used Today?

Cascarones are still used in Mexico. They have also become popular in certain parts of the United States.

In Mexico, cascarones are used in different celebrations. A really big one is a festival called Carnival. That festival happens in the spring.

The Mexican people also use cascarones on the Fifth of May. That day is an important day for Mexico. It celebrates the day Mexico became a country. It is like our Fourth of July celebration.

Cascarones can also be a part of a family's celebrations, like birthday parties and weddings.

So, what do you think? Would you like cascarones at your next party?

Now Try This

Cascarones are made from eggshells. But what about the leftover egg inside? Eggs are a very good food. Do you know any ways to cook eggs?

Think about the ways you might cook your eggs. Then talk with classmates and family about the different ways to cook eggs.

Now you are ready to make a cookbook about eggs.

Leftover Eggs

Glossary

celebrate *v.* to have a party for a special event or day

cherish *v.* to like or care about something or someone very deeply

China *n.* a large Asian country that is far from the United States

confetti *n.* tiny bits of brightly colored paper

decorate *v.* to fix something up to make it look special by painting, coloring, or trimming it with bits of things

empress *n.* a title for a woman who is the highest ruler of a country

Italy *n.* a country across the Atlantic Ocean from the United States

Mexico *n.* a country that shares the border with the southern part of the United States

perfume *n.* a liquid, like water, that smells sweet